Easy Cookbooks for Kids

for Kids

Easy Snacks
From Around the World

Heather Alexander

Enslow Elementary

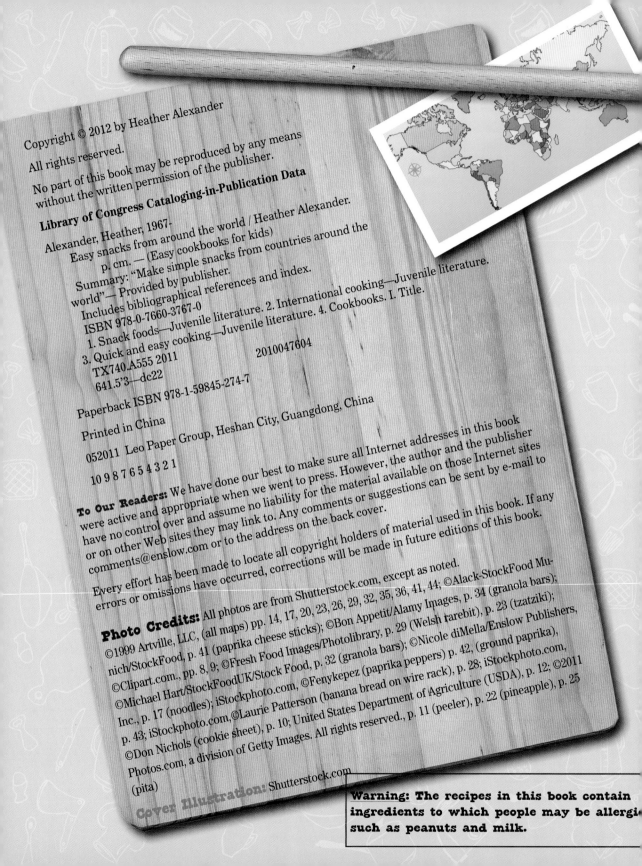

Library of Congress Cataloging-in-Publication Data

Alexander, Heather, 1967-
  Easy snacks from around the world / Heather Alexander.
    p. cm. — (Easy cookbooks for kids)
  Summary: "Make simple snacks from countries around the world"— Provided by publisher.
  Includes bibliographical references and index.
  ISBN 978-0-7660-3767-0
  1. Snack foods—Juvenile literature. 2. International cooking—Juvenile literature.
3. Quick and easy cooking—Juvenile literature. 4. Cookbooks. I. Title.
  TX740.A555 2011   2010047604
  641.5'3—dc22

Paperback ISBN 978-1-59845-274-7

Printed in China

052011 Leo Paper Group, Heshan City, Guangdong, China

10 9 8 7 6 5 4 3 2 1

To Our Readers: We have done our best to make sure all Internet addresses in this book were active and appropriate when we went to press. However, the author and the publisher have no control over and assume no liability for the material available on those Internet sites or on other Web sites they may link to. Any comments or suggestions can be sent by e-mail to comments@enslow.com or to the address on the back cover.

Every effort has been made to locate all copyright holders of material used in this book. If any errors or omissions have occurred, corrections will be made in future editions of this book.

Warning: The recipes in this book contain ingredients to which people may be allergic, such as peanuts and milk.

Contents

Introduction: Time to Cook

Have you ever met a kid from another country? Maybe you've seen pictures of kids from around the world. They probably seem very different from you. They may wear different clothes, speak a different language, or live in a different kind of house. But no matter what part of the world kids live in, they all get hungry—especially between meals. Snack time is a great time to have fun in the kitchen cooking something delicious to eat.

Food brings the world together. It tells a story about each country. Food can tell you about the country's climate and history, about the ingredients that are grown there, and about the way its people live. Cooking—and eating—are a fun and yummy way to learn about other cultures.

This cookbook has eleven recipes from eleven different countries or regions. When you follow a recipe, you can read about the country the dish comes from and the unique ingredients that flavor it.

Each recipe in this book has directions on **What You Need,** which lists the equipment and ingredients for the recipe, and a section called **Let's Cook!,** which tells you what to do. You will also find information on ingredients and techniques used.

So tie on an apron and let's cook easy snacks from all over the world!

Be Safe!

Whenever you are in the kitchen, there are important safety rules to follow.

1. Always **ask a responsible adult** for permission to cook. Always **have an adult** by your side when you use the oven, the stove, knives, or any appliance.

2. If you have long hair, tie it back. Remove dangling jewelry and tuck in any loose clothing.

3. Always use pot holders or oven mitts when handling anything on the stove or in the oven.

4. Never rush while cutting ingredients. You don't want the knife to slip.

5. If you are cooking something in the oven, stay in the house. Always use a timer—and stay where you can hear it.

6. If you are cooking something on the stove, stay in the kitchen.

7. ALLERGY ALERT! If you are cooking for someone else, let them know what ingredients you are using. Some people have life-threatening allergies to such foods as peanuts, dairy products, and shellfish.

Cooking Tips and Tricks

Keeping Clean:

- Wash your hands before you start. Make sure to also wash your hands after touching raw poultry, meat, or seafood and cracking eggs. These ingredients may have harmful germs that can make you very sick. Wash knives and cutting boards with soap and water after they've touched these ingredients.

- Use two cutting boards (one for meat and one for everything else) to avoid getting any germs from the meat on other food.

- Rinse all fruits and vegetables under cool water before you use them.

- Make sure your work space is clean before you start.

- Clean up as you cook.

Planning Ahead:

- Read the recipe from beginning to end before you start cooking. Make sure that you have all the ingredients and tools you will need before you start.

- If you don't understand something in a recipe, ask an adult for help.

Measuring:

- To measure dry ingredients, such as flour and sugar, dip the correct size measuring cup into the ingredient until it is full. Then level off the top of the cup with the flat side of a butter knife. Brown sugar is the only dry ingredient that should be tightly packed into a measuring cup.

- To measure liquid ingredients, such as milk and oil, use a clear glass or plastic measuring cup. Make sure it is on a flat surface. Pour the liquid into the cup until it reaches the correct level. Check the measurement at eye level.

- Remember that measuring spoons come in different sizes. Be sure you are using a *teaspoon* if the recipe asks for it and not a *tablespoon*.

Mixing:

- Beat—Mix ingredients together *fast* with a wooden spoon, whisk, or an electric mixer.

- Mix—Blend ingredients together with a wooden spoon, an electric mixer, or a whisk.

- Stir—Combine ingredients together with a wooden or metal spoon.

Cooking Basics:

- Cracking an egg—Hold the egg in one hand. Crack the eggshell against the side of a bowl. Using both hands, pull the eggshell apart over the bowl so the yolk and the white drop into the bowl.

- Cooling—After food has been baked in the oven, place it on a wire rack until it is no longer hot.

- Preheating—Turn the oven on at least 15 minutes before you need to use it.

- Warming ingredients—When a recipe says an ingredient should be at room temperature, take it out of the refrigerator for a while until it is no longer chilled.

- Greasing a pan—Spread butter, margarine, shortening, or oil over a baking pan or cookie sheet using a small piece of waxed paper. Or use a spray-on oil. It is often easier (and less messy) to cover a cookie sheet with parchment paper instead. You can find parchment paper in the baking aisle of your market.

- Greasing and flouring a pan—Grease a pan as described above. Then pour 1 or 2 tablespoons of flour onto the pan and shake it around so the entire surface is covered. Then hold the pan upside down over the sink or garbage can and tap the back of the pan gently so that the extra flour falls out.

Cooking Terms

Cooking has its own vocabulary. Here are some terms you should be familiar with.

chop (verb)—To cut into bite-sized pieces.

cuisine—The type of cooking used in a particular country or region.

dice (verb)—To cut into small pieces (smaller than chopped).

garlic bulb—A head of garlic, containing a number of smaller pieces, or garlic cloves.

mince (verb)—To cut into very small pieces.

scallion—Green onion.

shred—To tear into small pieces.

simmer—To boil slowly at a low temperature.

slice (verb)—To cut into thin pieces.

steam (verb)—To cook over simmering water.

Cooking Tools

broiler pan

cutting board

blender

colander

juicer

cookie sheet

measuring cups

loaf pan

oven mitt

measuring spoons

rubber spatula

paring knife

food processor

electric mixer

vegetable peeler

tongs

rolling pin

pizza cutter

steamer

saucepan

spatula

whisk

cooling rack

11

Nutrition

The best food is healthy as well as delicious. In planning meals, keep in mind the guidelines of the food pyramid.

MyPyramid
STEPS TO A HEALTHIER YOU
MyPyramid.gov

GRAINS	VEGETABLES	FRUITS	MILK	MEAT & BEANS

| GRAINS | VEGETABLES | FRUITS | MILK | MEAT & BEANS |
Make half your grains whole	Vary your veggies	Focus on fruits	Get your calcium-rich foods	Go lean with protein
Eat at least 3 oz. of whole-grain cereals, breads, crackers, rice, or pasta every day 1 oz. is about 1 slice of bread, about 1 cup of breakfast cereal, or 1/2 cup of cooked rice, cereal, or pasta	Eat more dark-green veggies like broccoli, spinach, and other dark leafy greens Eat more orange vegetables like carrots and sweet potatoes Eat more dry beans and peas like pinto beans, kidney beans, and lentils	Eat a variety of fruit Choose fresh, frozen, canned, or dried fruit Go easy on fruit juices	Go low-fat or fat-free when you choose milk, yogurt, and other milk products If you don't or can't consume milk, choose lactose-free products or other calcium sources such as fortified foods and beverages	Choose low-fat or lean meats and poultry Bake it, broil it, or grill it Vary your protein routine — choose more fish, beans, peas, nuts, and seeds

For a 2,000-calorie diet, you need the amounts below from each food group. To find the amounts that are right for you, go to MyPyramid.gov.

Eat 6 oz. every day	Eat 2 1/2 cups every day	Eat 2 cups every day	Get 3 cups every day; for kids aged 2 to 8, it's 2	Eat 5 1/2 oz. every day

Conversions

Recipes list amounts needed. Sometimes you need to know what that amount equals in another measurement. And sometimes you may want to make twice as much (or half as much) as the recipe yields. This chart will help you.

DRY INGREDIENT MEASUREMENTS	
Measure	**Equivalent**
1 tablespoon	3 teaspoons
¼ cup	4 tablespoons
½ cup	8 tablespoons
1 cup	16 tablespoons
2 cups	1 pound
½ stick of butter	¼ cup
1 stick of butter	½ cup
2 sticks of butter	1 cup
LIQUID INGREDIENT MEASUREMENTS	
8 fluid ounces	1 cup
1 pint (16 ounces)	2 cups
1 quart (2 pints)	4 cups
1 gallon (4 quarts)	16 cups

This book does not use abbreviations for measurements, but many cookbooks do. Here's what they mean:

c—cup

oz.—ounce

lb.—pound

T or tbsp.—tablespoon

t or tsp.—teaspoon

Chapter 1

Bruschetta

Bruschetta (*broo-SKEH-tuh*) is toasted bread topped with olive oil and garlicky tomatoes. It is a very popular snack and appetizer in Italy.

Italy

Italy is a country in the south of Europe. It is shaped like a boot. Italy is a peninsula, meaning it is surrounded on three sides by water. In the north, it is bordered by the snow-covered Alps Mountains.

Veggie Goodness

Italian cooking always uses the freshest ingredients, such as ripe, red tomatoes. Other popular Italian foods made with tomatoes are pizza and pasta with tomato sauce. This recipe also calls for scallions, which are sometimes called green onions. And it wouldn't be an Italian meal without garlic.

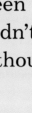

Did You Know?

A garlic bulb is made up of smaller sections called cloves. After you chop garlic, you can clean the garlicky smell off your hands with lemon juice.

What You Need

Equipment:
Small bowl
Sharp knife
Cutting board
Spoon

Ingredients:
3 large ripe tomatoes
2 scallions
½ teaspoon dried basil
1 clove garlic, peeled and minced
¼ teaspoon salt
3 tablespoons extra-virgin olive oil
1 long loaf Italian bread
4 basil leaves, chopped

What's This?
Olive oil comes from olives. Extra-virgin olive oil is the purest form.

Let's Cook!

1. Wash and dry tomatoes. Cut into quarters. Scoop out and throw away the seeds. Chop tomatoes into chunks and put into a bowl.

2. Wash, dry, and slice scallions. Add to bowl.

3. Add dried basil, garlic, salt, and olive oil. Stir. Chill in the refrigerator for a few hours, or overnight.

4. Cut bread into 1-inch slices. Toast in the toaster oven until lightly browned. (If you don't have a toaster oven, you can use a toaster or a regular oven for a few minutes.)

5. Scoop tomato mixture onto the bread. Tear the basil leaves into little pieces and sprinkle on top of the tomatoes. Serve right away.

Makes 4 serving.

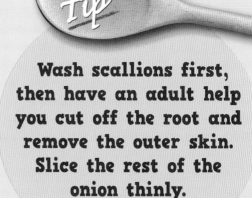

Cook's Tip

Wash scallions first, then have an adult help you cut off the root and remove the outer skin. Slice the rest of the onion thinly.

Cook's Tip

If you like the taste of garlic, rub a peeled garlic clove over the toasted bread before adding the tomato mixture.

Chapter 2

Cold Sesame Noodles

Chinese cuisine has many different ways to make noodles. These tangy sesame (*SESS-uh-mee*) noodles are eaten cold. It is often best to prepare them the day before and let them sit in the refrigerator overnight.

China

China is a large country in eastern Asia. China has the largest population in the world. One out of every five people on Earth lives in China.

The recipe for cold sesame noodles comes from the Hunan and Szechuan provinces of China.

Noodles

Noodles are never cut in China, because long noodles symbolize long life. They are traditionally served for birthday meals.

What You Need

Equipment:

1 large pot
Colander
1 large mixing bowl
1 medium mixing bowl
Whisk
Tongs (or 2 spoons)
Plastic baggie
Rolling pin
Cutting board
Knife
Aluminum foil or plastic wrap

Ingredients:

1 pound spaghetti or Soba noodles
4 tablespoons sesame oil
6 tablespoons peanut butter, smooth or chunky
3 tablespoons soy sauce
1 tablespoon of rice vinegar
2 tablespoons light brown sugar
1 teaspoon fresh ginger, minced
2 green onions, minced
¼ cup unsalted peanuts, chopped

Let's Cook!

1. Cook spaghetti according to the package directions. Drain in a colander. In a large bowl, toss spaghetti with 2 tablespoons of sesame oil. Cover and refrigerate for at least 1 hour.

2. In a medium bowl, whisk together 2 tablespoons of sesame oil, peanut butter, soy sauce, rice vinegar, sugar, and ginger until smooth.

3. Pour sauce on cold spaghetti and toss with tongs or 2 spoons until the noodles are completely coated.

4. Cover and refrigerate for at least 1 hour.

5. Put peanuts in a plastic baggie and zip it closed. Using a rolling pin, roll over baggie until peanuts inside are crushed. Sprinkle crushed peanuts and diced scallions on top of cold noodles when ready to serve.

Makes 8 servings.

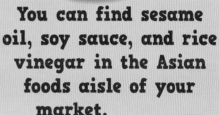

Cook's Tip

You can find sesame oil, soy sauce, and rice vinegar in the Asian foods aisle of your market.

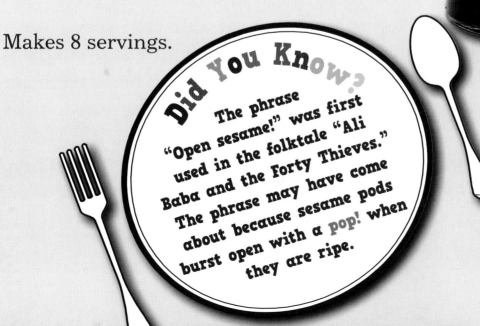

Did You Know?

The phrase "Open sesame!" was first used in the folktale "Ali Baba and the Forty Thieves." The phrase may have come about because sesame pods burst open with a pop! when they are ripe.

19

Chapter 3

Caribbean Fruit Smoothie

What hits the spot on a hot, sunny day in the Caribbean islands? An ice-cold fruit smoothie, of course!

Caribbean Islands

There are more than seven thousand islands in the Caribbean. The islands are all different sizes, with beautiful sandy beaches, turquoise water, and tall palm trees. The Caribbean islands are surrounded by the Atlantic Ocean and the Caribbean Sea.

20

Tropical Fruit

Tropical fruits, such as pineapples, coconuts, mangoes, and guava, are grown in the Caribbean. The warm trade winds and mild temperatures allow these sweet fruits, many rich in vitamin C, to bloom all year long.

What You Need

Equipment:
Electric blender
Cutting board
Sharp knife

Ingredients:
1 large banana, peeled and broken into pieces
½ cup mango, peeled and diced
½ cup orange juice
½ cup pineapple juice
½ cup ice cubes

What's This?

A mango is a large fruit. You can't eat the tough skin, but the juicy orange fruit inside is very sweet.

Cook's Tip

If you don't have fresh mango, you can use canned mango.

Let's Cook!

1. Combine all fruits and juices in the blender.

2. With an adult's help, mix on medium-high speed for 1 minute.

3. Add ice cubes and blend for 2 minutes until frothy. Pour into tall glasses.

Makes 3–4 servings.

Did You Know?

Pineapple was first called "anana," a Caribbean word that means "excellent fruit."

Chapter 4

Tzatziki

Tzatziki (*dza-DZEE-kee*) is a Greek dip made with thick yogurt and chopped cucumber. It is always served cold. Tzatziki is often served as a "meze," which means "appetizer" in Greek, but it makes a great healthy snack.

Greece

Greece is a peninsula in southern Europe. It is surrounded on three sides by the Mediterranean Sea, the Aegean Sea, and the Ionian Sea. Its land is very rocky. Because it is so near the sea, Greek food often includes a lot of seafood.

What You Need

Equipment:
Vegetable peeler
Cutting board
Knife
Spoon
Small bowl
Plastic wrap

Ingredients:
1 medium cucumber
1 clove garlic, peeled and minced
2 green onions
2 teaspoons olive oil
1 teaspoon fresh or dried dill weed
2 teaspoons lemon juice
1½ cup (12 ounces) Greek-style plain yogurt

Kirby

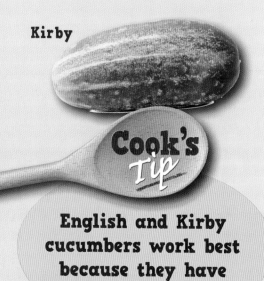

Cook's Tip

English and Kirby cucumbers work best because they have very few seeds.

English

What's This?

Greek yogurt is a thick, full-fat yogurt. You can usually find it in your market's dairy section. Do not use regular yogurt for tzatziki, because it is not creamy enough.

Let's Cook!

1. With an adult's help, peel the cucumber. Cut the peeled cucumber in half lengthwise. Using a small spoon, scoop out the seeds and throw them away. Cut the cucumber into tiny chunks. Put the cucumber chunks into a small bowl.

2. Add the diced garlic clove to the bowl. Wash, dry, and finely chop the green onions. Add to the bowl.

3. Add olive oil, lemon juice, and dill. Add yogurt and mix well.

4. Cover the bowl with plastic wrap. Chill in the refrigerator for at least 1 hour.

5. Serve as a dip for warm pita or cut vegetables.

Makes 4–6 servings.

Cook's Tip

After cutting the cucumber, press the chunks between two sheets of paper towel to get all the extra moisture out. Cucumbers contain a lot of water.

Chapter 5

Banana Bread

Banana bread is a sweet cake-like bread from Central America that's easy to make. The sweetness comes from mashed yellow bananas.

Central America

Bananas grow in Costa Rica, Honduras, and Guatemala in Central America, a narrow piece of land that connects North America and South America. Central America has a warm tropical climate, which is perfect for growing bananas.

Bananas

Bananas are picked while their skin, or peel, is green if they are being shipped to other countries. A banana is ripe when its peel is bright yellow, and overripe when its peel turns brown. For this recipe, it's okay to use bananas that are a bit overripe—it will make the dish sweeter.

What You Need

Equipment:

Large mixing bowl
Small bowl
Wooden spoon
Fork
Electric mixer
8" x 4" loaf pan
Wire cooling rack

Ingredients:

1¾ cups all-purpose flour
⅔ cup sugar
2 teaspoons baking powder
½ teaspoon baking soda
¼ teaspoon salt
½ teaspoon ground cinnamon
3 ripe medium-sized bananas
⅓ cup butter or margarine
2 tablespoons milk
2 eggs

Cook's Tip

Try adding ½ cup of chopped nuts, chocolate chips, or dried fruit to your banana bread batter.

Let's Cook!

1. Preheat oven to 350°F (180°C).
2. In a large bowl, combine flour, sugar, baking powder, baking soda, salt, and cinnamon.
3. In a small bowl, mash the peeled bananas. Add mashed bananas to dry ingredients.
4. Add milk and butter to the bowl and with an adult's help, beat with an electric mixer until blended. Add eggs and beat until smooth.
5. Pour batter into greased loaf pan. Bake for 50–55 minutes.
6. Remove pan from oven using oven mitts and cool for ten minutes on a wire rack. Then, insert a butter knife between the bread and the side of the pan. You should be able to pry the bread out of the pan gently. Cool the bread completely on the wire rack. Slice and serve.

Makes 3–4 servings.

What's This?

To mash a peeled banana, use the back of a fork or a spoon to press the fruit, or use a potato masher.

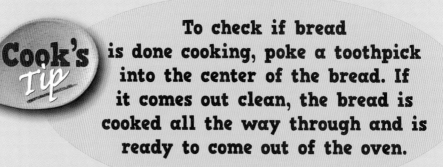

Cook's Tip

To check if bread is done cooking, poke a toothpick into the center of the bread. If it comes out clean, the bread is cooked all the way through and is ready to come out of the oven.

Chapter 6

Welsh Rarebit

Welsh rarebit is a traditional snack from Wales. Thick cheese sauce with a hint of spice is broiled on toast. This open-face sandwich is a favorite late-night treat.

According to legends, the dish used to be called "Welsh Rabbit." Back in the 1700s, when people caught and ate rabbits for dinner, the Welsh were said to be bad at catching rabbits. People joked that the cheese on toast they ate was really "Welsh Rabbit." Over the years, the name changed a bit.

Wales

Wales, along with England, Scotland, and Northern Ireland, make up the United Kingdom. Wales has one of the longest single names for a city: **Llanfairpwllgwyngyllgogerychwyrndrobwllllantysiliogogogoch.**

What You Need

Equipment:

Medium saucepan

Large spoon

Paring knife

Cutting board

Broiler pan or baking pan

Aluminum foil

Ingredients:

4 slices of bread (sourdough works well)

2 eggs, beaten

8 ounces grated Cheddar cheese

1 teaspoon Worcestershire sauce

2 teaspoons Dijon mustard

1 tablespoon butter

4 tablespoons milk

1 ripe tomato, sliced

What's This?

Dijon (*dee-ZHON*) mustard is a highly seasoned, light brown mustard. It was first made in Dijon, France. Do not use yellow American mustard as a substitute.

Let's Cook!

1. In medium saucepan, combine beaten eggs, milk, butter, mustard, and Worcestershire sauce over low heat. Mix well for 3 minutes.

2. Slowly add in cheese, one handful at a time, mixing well in between additions so the cheese melts. Make sure the sauce does not boil. Stir for 5–7 minutes until the sauce becomes thick.

3. Toast the bread. Line a broiler or baking pan with aluminum foil. Preheat oven to broil.

4. Place bread on the pan and place tomato slices on the bread. Spoon the cheese sauce over the tomatoes. Broil until the cheese bubbles and starts turning brown. Remove from the oven and serve warm.

   Makes 4 servings.

Cook's Tip

When heating milk on the stove, always keep the heat low and stir, so the milk doesn't boil over or burn.

Did You Know?

In 1837, two men in Worcester, England, created a special sauce made with vinegar and spices. They named it Worcestershire (WUSS-ta-sheer) sauce, and they wouldn't tell anyone the recipe. The recipe is still a secret today.

31

Chapter 7

Granola Bars

Granola bars are made of rolled oats and lots of other yummy things. They can contain honey, dried fruit, nuts, and chocolate chips. They are a popular on-the-go snack, since they are easy to carry when you are going somewhere. Granola bars were created in the United States in the 1970s.

Granola bars come in many different flavors. The great thing about baking them yourself is that you get to choose what you want in your granola bar.

United States

The United States is a country that has forty-nine states in North America and the state of Hawaii in the Pacific Ocean. Its capital is Washington, D.C.

What You Need

Equipment:

Large mixing bowl

Wooden spoon

9"x 13" pan

Sharp knife

Ingredients:

3 cups old-fashioned rolled oats

1½ cups crispy rice cereal

½ cup all-purpose or whole wheat flour

1 teaspoon baking soda

½ cup brown sugar

½ cup chocolate chips

½ cup raisins

¼ teaspoon cinnamon

1 egg

1 teaspoon vanilla extract

½ cup (1 stick) unsalted butter at room temperature

Cook's Tip

Be creative! You can also add peanuts, chopped almonds, dried cranberries, shredded coconut, or mini marshmallows.

What's This?

Rolled oats are made from oat grain that has been flattened between rollers. You can use use Quaker Oats or another plain oatmeal.

What's This?

Whole wheat flour is light brown. It has more fiber than white flour.

Let's Cook!

1. Preheat oven to 350°F (180°C).

2. Grease 9" x 13" pan.

3. Stir together all dry ingredients in a large bowl. Then add all wet ingredients. Mix well.

4. Spoon mixture into greased pan. Pat the mixture down well with the back of the spoon or your clean hands to make sure it is spread out evenly and packed tightly.

5. Bake for 18–20 minutes. Remove from oven with oven mitts or pot holders. Cool for 10 minutes, and then use a knife to cut into bars.

6. Cool completely and let the bars sit for 1 hour before serving. Wrap bars in plastic wrap to store.

Makes 15–20 bars.

Chapter 8

Guacamole

Guacamole (*gwahk-ah-MOLE-lee*) is a dip from Mexico made with mashed avocados and served with tortilla chips. In many Mexican restaurants, guacamole is served in a molcajete (mole-ca-HAY-tay), a mortar and pestle made from lava stone (but don't worry—a regular bowl works just fine!)

Mexico

Mexico is a country in North America that borders the United States. Its capital, Mexico City, is one of the largest cities in the world.

Guacamole was created by the ancient Aztec who lived in Mexico many centuries ago.

What You Need

Equipment:

Knife

Cutting board

Spoon

Fork

Medium mixing bowl

Ingredients:

3 ripe avocados

Bag of tortilla chips

1 medium-sized ripe tomato

½ small onion

2 cloves garlic, peeled

2 teaspoons ground cumin

1 small fresh jalapeño pepper (optional)

1 lime

What's This?

Jalapeño (*hal-uh-PAIN-yo*) peppers are spicy chili peppers from Mexico. Add these only if you like spicy foods.

Did You Know?

Avocados are sometimes called "poor man's butter," because the mashed fruit is so creamy.

Let's Cook!

1. Ask an adult to help you cut the avocados in half lengthwise, cutting around the large pits. Scoop out the pits with a spoon and throw them away. Then scoop out the green insides and put them in the mixing bowl. Throw away the outer skin. Use the back of a fork to mash the green avocado insides.

2. Wash the tomato and remove the stem. Cut into tiny chunks and add to the bowl.

3. Mince the onion and garlic and add to the bowl. Add the cumin. Mince the jalapeño pepper, if you want to include it. Stir well. Cut the lime in half and squeeze the juice into the bowl (watch that the seeds don't go in too). Stir well.

4. Pour the guacamole into a serving dish. Eat the guacamole with tortilla chips.

Makes 4–6 servings

Chapter 9

Hummus

Hummus (*HUM-us*) is a Middle Eastern spread made from mashed chickpeas, olive oil, garlic, and seasonings. It is usually scooped up and eaten with flatbread, or pita.

Middle East

Iraq, Israel, Jordan, Lebanon, Saudi Arabia, and Syria are some of the countries that make up the Middle East. Part of the Middle East is in northern Africa and part is in southwestern Asia. These ancient desert lands are surrounded by the Persian Gulf, the Arabian Sea, and the Mediterranean Sea.

Chickpeas

Chickpeas are round, beige beans. The word "hummus" in Arabic means "chickpea." Hummus is one of the oldest foods. It has been eaten in Egypt for over seven thousand years!

What You Need

Equipment:

Food processor or blender

Rubber spatula

Ingredients:

1 15-ounce can of chickpeas, drained

1 clove of garlic

2 teaspoons ground cumin

½ teaspoon salt

2 tablespoons olive oil

2 tablespoons lemon juice

Cook's Tip

Chickpeas are also called garbanzo beans or ceci (CHEH-chee).

What's This?

Cumin (*CYU-min*) is a spice from the Middle East. It was used by the ancient Egyptians as medicine.

Let's Cook!

1. In food processor or blender, combine all ingredients. Blend until smooth. (Get an adult's help with this step.)

2. Using a rubber spatula, scoop hummus into a bowl and cover. Refrigerate for 1–2 hours. Serve with raw celery or carrots, crackers, or pita.

Makes 4–6 servings.

Cook's Tip

To make crispy pita chips, cut pita into triangles, brush with olive oil, and toast for 10 minutes in a 400°F (205°C) oven.

Chapter 10

Paprika Cheese Sticks

These cheesy bread sticks from Hungary make a great snack. This recipe uses cheddar cheese, but you can make them with all different kinds of cheeses.

Hungary

Hungary is a country in central Europe. Its capital, Budapest, is really two cities. Buda is on one side of the Danube River, and Pest is on the other side.

Paprika

Hungary is one of the largest producers of paprika. Paprika is a spice made from dried peppers. Because of its red-orange color, paprika is used not only to season foods but also to give them color.

What You Need

Equipment:
Parchment paper
Medium mixing bowl
Wooden spoon
Rolling pin
Pizza cutter
2 cookie sheets
Wire rack

Ingredients:
1½ cups all-purpose flour
½ cup (1 stick) butter or margarine at room temperature
2 cups shredded sharp cheddar cheese at room temperature
1 teaspoon baking powder
1 teaspoon paprika
½ teaspoon salt
½ cup water
Grated parmesan cheese

What's This?

The longer cheese is "aged" before it is sold, the sharper, or stronger, its flavor will be.

Cook's Tip

You can use either packaged parmesan cheese (sold with pastas and tomato sauces) or fresh parmesan cheese (in the dairy aisle).

Let's Cook!

1. Preheat oven to 400°F (205°C). Grease or line two cookie sheets with parchment paper.

2. In a medium bowl, combine flour, butter, cheddar cheese, baking powder, paprika, and salt. Slowly add the water, stirring all the while, to form the dough.

3. With clean hands, shape the dough into a ball. Sprinkle some flour on a clean, flat surface. With a rolling pin, roll out the dough until it is ¼-inch thick. Use a pizza cutter to cut dough into sticks about 5 inches long.

Cook's Tip

Dough gets tough if you handle it too much. Do the minimum amount of shaping you need to make a ball.

4. Place sticks 1 inch apart on prepared cookie sheets. Gently hold each end of the stick and twist twice to give the stick a spiral-like look.

5. Sprinkle sticks with a little parmesan cheese and some more paprika.

6. Bake for 8-10 minutes or until lightly browned. Remove from the oven using oven mitts and cool on a wire rack. Serve warm.

Makes 24 sticks.

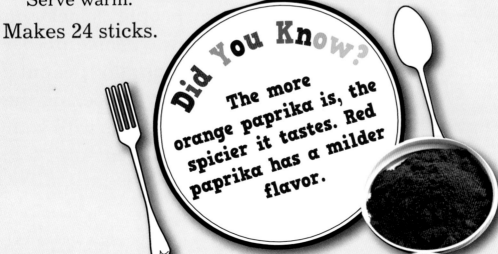

Did You Know?

The more orange paprika is, the spicier it tastes. Red paprika has a milder flavor.

Chapter 11

Edamame

Edamame (*eh-dah-MAh-may*) is a vegetable from Japan that's both nutritious and great tasting. These salted green soybeans can be served hot or cold.

Japan

Japan is a country of over three thousand islands in the Pacific Ocean off the east coast of Asia. It is often called "The Land of the Rising Sun." It has beautiful buildings and gardens.

"Edamame" means "beans of branches" in Japanese. In Japan, people snack on edamame the way people in other countries snack on peanuts. You eat them by squeezing the beans out of the pods with your fingers. Each pod contains two or three delicious beans.

HOKKAIDO

JAPAN

HONSHU Tokyo

SHIKOKU

KYUSHU

What You Need

Equipment:

Large pot

Vegetable steamer

Bowl

Ingredients:

1 pound frozen edamame in the pods

2 teaspoons kosher salt

1 teaspoon sesame oil

What's This?

A vegetable steamer sits in a pot of boiling or simmering water holding the vegetables. It allows them to cook and stay crisp.

What's This?

Kosher salt is coarser than ordinary table salt—that is, it has bigger grains. You can use table salt if kosher salt is not available.

Did You Know?

Edamame pods are not edible. Only the beans can be eaten.

Let's Cook!

1. Place frozen edamame in vegetable steamer. Boil the water and steam for 5 minutes.
2. Pour cooked edamame into a large bowl. Sprinkle with sesame oil and kosher salt. Stir gently and serve warm.

Makes 4 servings.

Cook's Tip

You can make your own steamer. Use a large pot and a footed metal colander that fits inside. Fill the pot with only enough water so it doesn't reach the colander. Put your vegetables in the colander. The steam from the boiling water in the pot will cook them.

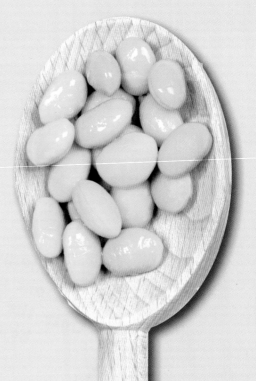

Further Reading

Books

D'Amico, Joan, and Karen Eich Drummond. *The Coming to America Cookbook: Delicious Recipes and Fascinating Stories from America's Many Cultures.* Hoboken, N.J.: John Wiley & Sons, Inc., 2005.

De Mariaffi, Elisabeth. *Eat It Up! Lip-Smacking Recipes for Kids.* Toronto: Owlkids, 2009.

Dodge, Abigail Johnson. *Around the World Cookbook.* New York: DK Publishing, 2008.

Lagasse, Emeril. *Emeril's There's a Chef in My World!: Recipes That Take You Places.* New York: HarperCollins Publishers, 2006.

Wagner, Lisa. *Cool Sweets & Treats to Eat: Easy Recipes for Kids to Cook.* Edina, Minn.: ABDO Publishing Co., 2007.

Internet Addresses

Cookalotamus Kids

<http://www.cookalotamus.com/kids.html>

PBS Kids: Cafe Zoom

<http://pbskids.org/zoom/activities/cafe/>

Spatulatta.com

<http://www.spatulatta.com/>

Index